YOUR KNOWLEDGE HAS VALUE

- We will publish your bachelor's and master's thesis, essays and papers

- Your own eBook and book - sold worldwide in all relevant shops

- Earn money with each sale

Upload your text at www.GRIN.com and publish for free

G R I N

Remi Bauer

Aus der Reihe: e-fellows.net stipendiaten-wissen

e-fellows.net (Hrsg.)

Band 874

Teenage Rampage. School shootings

GRIN Verlag

Bibliografische Information der Deutschen Nationalbibliothek:

Die Deutsche Bibliothek verzeichnet diese Publikation in der Deutschen National-
bibliografie; detaillierte bibliografische Daten sind im Internet über http://dnb.d-
nb.de/ abrufbar.

Imprint:

Copyright © 2007 GRIN Verlag GmbH
Druck und Bindung: Books on Demand GmbH, Norderstedt Germany
ISBN: 978-3-656-56553-6

This book at GRIN:

http://www.grin.com/en/e-book/266434/teenage-rampage-school-shootings

GRIN - Your knowledge has value

Der GRIN Verlag publiziert seit 1998 wissenschaftliche Arbeiten von Studenten, Hochschullehrern und anderen Akademikern als eBook und gedrucktes Buch. Die Verlagswebsite www.grin.com ist die ideale Plattform zur Veröffentlichung von Hausarbeiten, Abschlussarbeiten, wissenschaftlichen Aufsätzen, Dissertationen und Fachbüchern.

Table of Contents

1. Introduction

"After I mow down a whole area full of you snotty-ass rich motherfucker high-strung God-like-attitude-having worthless pieces of shit whores, I don't care if I live or die."[1] With provocative quotes like this one, Eric Harris announced his merciless school shooting. Together with Dylan Klebold, he committed the Columbine massacre - the worst carnage ever perpetrated by teenagers in the United States. On 18 April, 1999, the two youngsters entered Columbine High School in Littleton, Colorado, heavily armed.[2] Their arsenal included "two sawn off shotguns, [a] 9mm Hi-Point carbine rifle, [a] TEC-DC-9 semi-automatic pistol and a total of 95 explosive devices."[3] Regardless of the consequences Harris and Klebold methodically killed their fellow students. A total of thirteen dead and twenty-three wounded people was the sad result of this atrocious act.[4] After the bloodbath the American people wondered why warning signs were not taken serious and how such a bloody deed could take place in a suburban area in Colorado. Even so, the Columbine massacre was not a singular instance, it was the incident that

Dylan Klebold (top) and Eric Harris[1]

drew attention to school shootings. Before the deadly homicide Eric Harris recorded a message saying "People will die because of me ... It will be a day that will be remembered forever."[5] Tragically, he was proved right. People all over the world kept the shooting in mind and, in addition to it, the idiom 'pull a Columbine' was append to the American encyclopedia.[6] Because of the fatal carnage, people became aware of a big problem in society. There have been heated controversies about the homicides themselves questioning if the legal custodian, violent music, weapons of the shooters or the system of cliques which is part of the normal high school life should be blamed.[7] Also, the aftermaths of the schoolyard shootings and prevention methods which should be introduced were discussed in public. The following paper will give a valuable insight into the topic.

---

[1] Mendoza, Antonio (2002, pg. 123).
[2] Cf. Lane, Brian and Gregg, Wilfred (2004, pg. 73 f.).
[3] Mendoza, Antonio (2002, pg. 123).
[4] Cf. Lane, Brian and Gregg, Wilfred (2004, pg. 73 f.).
[5] Brooks, Brown and Merritt, Rob. No Easy Answers: The Truth Behind Death at Columbine (2002, pg. 124).
[6] Cf. Mendoza, Antonio (2002, pg. 123).
[7] Cf. Gibbs, Nancy. ...In Sorrow and Disbelief (1999, Vol. 153 No. 17; pg. 25 f.).

2. Shootings

2.1. Definition of a school shooting

A carnage must involve certain factors to be defined as a school shooting. For one thing, it must "take place on a school-related stage before an audience."[8] Secondly, the killing must incriminate multiple victims, some of whom are only shot because of their figurative importance or haphazardly. Thus, the perpetrator must attempt to commit a mass murder by killing as many people as possible. Hence, homicides with single targets are not recognized as school shootings even so they occur on an education places. Additionally, such an event has to be committed by one or more shooters who are pupils or former students of the school. According to this definition carnages committed by outsiders are not determined as school shootings.[9]

2.2 History of school shootings

School shootings existed long before Columbine. Already in the 1980's such events took place. For instance, fourteen-year-old James Alan Kearbey entered his Junior high school armed with guns and "killed the school principal, and wounded two teachers and a student."[10] This tragic occurrence happened in 1985 and made the Goddard Junior High School students in Kansas to one of the first witnesses of a problem which just started to spread all over the United States.[11] In "Rampage: The Social Roots of School Shootings" a diagram shows the number of school shootings in the period from 1974 to 2002.[12] As one can observe, shootings occurred scarcely until 1989. Merely six attacks took place within fifteen school years. Bloodbaths on school grounds have experienced a boost in the 1990's. In the year 1997-1998 the number of schoolyard shootings was culminating with a total of six homicides. Fortunately, in the following years the count decreased again. The diagram also exposes the number of attacks plus post-Columbine plots since 1999. This displays the actions which were disclosed by police and school officials after the deadly Columbine massacre. It is impossible to know if these plots would have concluded with lethal homicides and many victims or would have stayed a perverse fancy in a youngsters mind. "Either way they are particularly reassuring: students are still thinking about, planning and moving to

---

[8] Newman, Katherine S. and Fox, Cybelle and Roth, Wendy (2002, pg.50).
[9] Cf. Newman, Katherine S. and Fox, Cybelle and Roth, Wendy (2002, pg.50).
[10] Mendoza, Antonio (2002, pg. 14).
[11] Cf. Mendoza, Antonio (2002, pg. 14).
[12] Cf. Appendix: Rampage: The Social Roots of School Shootings.

execute rampage shootings."[13] The attempted mass murder on a schoolyard in Emsdetten, Germany, on November 20, 2006, when a teenager wounded five students before killing himself, shows that this propensity is still up-to-date.[14] Also, the threats that followed, after this incident was made public, are shocking.[15] This school homicide also indicates that teenage carnages are not only a problem of American society. Even though most shootings took place in the United States, in the last years they occurred more frequently in other countries, too. Some non-American nations have shocking records. For example, the worst bloodbath on an education place ever perpetrated by a youngster took place in Erfurt, Germany. On April 26, 2002, nineteen-year-old Robert Steinhäuser entered the Johann Gutenberg Gymnasium armed and masked, after he was expelled from the school in February. His arsenal included a pistol and a deadly shotgun. Belonging to two gun clubs, Steinhäuser was an excellent marksman. Since his deadly carnage pertained his former teachers, Robert chased them. In consequence he killed one policeman, two

Robert Steinhäuser[2]

students and a dismaying number of thirteen teachers before committing suicide.[16] With a total of sixteen dead victims, the German student slew more people than the Columbine shooters. Ever since horrifying stories like Erfurt or Columbine hit the headlines, experts are reflecting about the causes for the bloody deeds.

2.3 Causes of school shootings

2.3.1 Mental Illnesses

Firstly, a mental illness can be the cause of a school shooting. The problem in finding a direct influence is that only a few shooters are diagnosed mentally ill before their carnage. An undetected insanity can be problematical, because it is not a conspicuous warning sign. However, "many are discovered afterward to be mentally ill."[17] Those shooters need diverse ranges of treatment after their crimes. It is possible that the teenagers are going to be suicidal for a major part of their lives. Also, presumably they will sustain iterated flashbacks

[13] Newman, Katherine S. and Fox, Cybelle and Roth, Wendy (2002, pg.51).
[14] Cf. Pleigen, Fritz. Emsdetten: Amoklauf war lange geplant (06/01/2007).
[15] Cf. Polizei Minden-Lübbecke. Trittbrettfahrer nach Amoklauf von Emsdetten beschäftigten auch die Polizei in Minden (06/01/2007).
[16] Cf. Lane, Brian and Gregg, Wilfred (2004, pg. 317).
[17] Newman, Katherine S. and Fox, Cybelle and Roth, Wendy (2002, pg.59).

to the day of their shooting.[18] But yet there are cases in which gunners were known to be laid up with mental illnesses. Most specifically those maladies are depression and schizophrenia. In these cases the students were treated by psychiatrists with different drugs such as Zoloft, Prozac, Paxil and Luvox. These antidepressants have various adverse reactions.[19] "The following side effects are listed for Prozac: apathy; hallucinations; hostility; irrational ideas; paranoid reactions; antisocial behavior; hysteria; and suicidal thoughts."[20] Therefore, conjectures have been made that the drugs, which were prescribed by doctors, could be linked directly to the teenage rampages. Nevertheless one has to be careful with assumptions like that, since more then two million people in the United States are affected with schizophrenia. In most cases the illness developed during their adolescence.[21] Hence one can say that the number of school shootings is incommensurable to the number of juveniles treated with antidepressants.

2.3.2 Social trouble

Another possible cause for the school shootings can be social trouble. These social problems can be family difficulties such as parent's "divorce or sexual abuse, frequent relocations, and fragile family relationships as well as lack of awareness or involvement [of parents] in children's lives."[22] Based on these reasons one may wonder if parents should be held responsible for their sons' and daughters' behaviors. If warning signs are ignored or dismissed, society blames the parents asking themselves why the bloody deeds were not stopped and where the parents were.[23] These familiar troubles can result in antisocial behavior and, therefore, the students are more likely to become outsiders. Not only family problems are covered by the factor social trouble but also bullying at school. If a teenager does not belong to a famous group at school, such as cheerleaders or sport teams, he is treated like an outsider. Youngsters are psychologically frail. They do not know how to deal with rejection. Assaults and battery, mistreatment and violation leave one's mark on a teenager. Consequently "kids who feel powerless and rejected are capable of doing horrible things."[24] For the students' troubles at their education place "school[s] came in for criticism as well."[25] They were blistered to be too large and for that reason too impersonal. Thus, teachers and administrators are not able to pay as much attention to students as they

---

[18] Roche, Timothy and Bower, Amanda. Young Voices from the Cell (08/08/2006).
[19] Cf. Mendoza, Antonio (2002, pg. 8 f.).
[20] Mendoza, Antonio (2002, pg. 8 f.).
[21] Cf. Newman, Katherine S. and Fox, Cybelle and Roth, Wendy (2002, pg. 60).
[22] Cf. Newman, Katherine S. and Fox, Cybelle and Roth, Wendy (2002, pg. 62).
[23] Cf. Dickinson, Amy. Where Were the Parents? (1999, Vol. 153 No. 17; pg. 40.).
[24] Cohen, Adam. A Curse of Cliques (1999, Vol. 153 No. 17; pg. 45).
[25] Carter, Green Lee (2002, pg. 521).

demand. Consequential, some youngsters are lost and left alone at their schools and warning signs remain unnoticed. The lack of communication between students and teachers is animadverted, as well. Naught of significance is conveyed from a teenager to the older generation anymore. Thereby, the detection of premonition features is aggravated.[26] This shows very plainly, that the milieu and the social periphery influence teenagers a lot and they are also part of unmasking warning signs. If the assessment of warning signs does not work or when social trouble negatively influence a teenager, it can be a factor for the youngster to commit a deadly crime at his or her school.

2.3.3 Gun availability

In addition, gun availability is a topic often discussed closely linked to school shootings. Society wonders if weapons are to blame for the teenage rampages. Gun activists demanded stricter laws to limit the access to firearms by introducing tougher firearm specifications.[27] Due to the fact that the activists believe that "it is foolish to think that we can reduce gun violence among young people without reducing their easy access to weapons"[28], they charge the gun availability for the school homicides. Studies show that most of the shooters got their firearms because they were stored irresponsibly in the parental home or a friend's house.[29] The high number of guns in American houses enables the children to gain access easily. There exist circa two hundred million guns in the United States which are possessed by peradventure thirty-five percent of all American ménages. The existence of these weapons influences the lives of the American people. With a substantial number of guns the number of murder and suicide increases. The prospect that an instant of fury will terminate in an injury or in death is more likely when a weapon is being gamed. Many humans are dying yearly, and, in fact, more people are losing friends and family. Exceedingly, the guns which revolve in society impinge on youngsters. Firearms are the weapon for homicide as well as suicide.[30] Thus, one can say that the subsistence of guns in American society is a factor that most school shootings are committed in the United States. Yet, school homicide also happen in countries with stricter gun laws like Germany. Germany has one of the most severe laws concerning guns. While in America only a driver's license is needed to buy or to posses a firearm, Germans must evince their 'need' as well as pass a

---

[26] Cf. Carter, Green Lee (2002, pg. 521 f.).
[27] Cf. "The School Shootings: Are Guns to Blame?." Issues & Controversies On File 29 May 1998.
[28] "The School Shootings: Are Guns to Blame?." Issues & Controversies On File 29 May 1998.
[29] Cf. Carter, Green Lee (2002, pg. 521).
[30] Cf. Embar, Wanda. Gun availability (10/01/2007).

government test.[31] In defiance of the strict gun laws, the worst school shooting ever was committed in Germany.[32] All in all, it suggests itself that the access to weaponry is connected to school shootings. Notwithstanding, in hindsight, we will never know if the perpetrators would have committed their assaults without having guns available so easily.

2.3.4 Violent media

Moreover, violent media can be a cause for school shootings. All youngsters are exposed to violent movies, extreme music and rowdyish homepages on the internet. Vengeance fantasies are rambling in movies. Brutal films do inspire some children to commit vicious bloodbaths at school. For instance, the movie "Natural Born Killers" which tells the story of two teenagers traveling through the Southwest conducting psychedelic mass-slaughters was studied by the Columbine shooters.[33] Also violent games like "Doom" and "Quake" hit the headlines after school shootings were committed. These crunch encounters are first-person shooter games and are known for the wide range of arsenal which is available for the players. Yet, it is not possible to calculate the effect the games and the movies had on the gunners in retrospect.[34] Nevertheless, a 2003 study reveals that playing violent video games in a young age can trigger aggressiveness in one's behavior in later years. Likewise, researches have evicted a twelve percent raise in aggressive behavioral problems after watching violent television. Also, children who watch television shows and films for more than four hours a day, have to face other problems than being exposed to violent media. Inquests have shown that heavy viewers "put in less effort at school, have poorer reading skills, play less friendly with friends, have fewer hobbies and activities, and are more likely to be overweight."[35] This can constitute the children to outsiders. Overall, one can say that studies showed that there are three main implications of playing rowdyish video games and watching brutal television shows. Firstly, children may become less sensible to the ache, agony and affliction of others. Secondly, minors could be more timorous and afraid of their surroundings. And thirdly, youngsters might be more presumably to behaving thuggish, violent or hurtful toward other people.[36] In connection with school shootings violent music was mentioned as well. Especially the name of the "self-proclaimed Antichrist superstar Marilyn Manson"[37] hit the headlines. The Columbine killers listened to Marilyn Manson's rock songs which

---

[31] Cf. National Rifle Association of America, Institute for Legislative Action. Gun Laws, Culture, Justice & Crime in Foreign Countries (10/01/2007).
[32] Cf. Lane, Brian and Gregg, Wilfred (2004, pg. 317).
[33] Cf. Corliss, Richard. Bang, You're Dead (1999 Vol. 153 No. 17; pg. 49 f.).
[34] Cf. Taylor, Chris. Digital Dungeons. (1999 Vol. 153 No. 17; pg. 50).
[35] Tompkins, Aimee. The Psychological Effects of Violent Media on Children (07/01/2007).
[36] Cf. Tompkins. The Psychological Effects of Violent Media on Children (07/01/2007).
[37] Corliss, Richard. Bang, You're Dead (1999 Vol. 153 No. 17; pg. 49).

according to the press promote death, hate, suicide, drugs and Columbine-like behavior. Yet, the musician doubts that his influence is as big as the media alleges. He rather believes that the President and the real world have their effects on youngsters. In an interview with filmmaker Michael Moore, he states that watching the news radiates fear since stories about floods, wars, AIDS and murder are reported.[38] The superstar encapsulates the most important fact, neither one can really tell to what extend violent media influences a child, nor can anyone tell if it is news stories or brutal music which transforms a ordinary teenager into a mass murder. Almost every teenager in the world is confronted with violent media but doubtless only the least of all are thinking about committing a schoolyard shooting.

2.3.5 Combinations of factors

Recapitulating, one can say that there is not a single reason for a shooter to commit a school homicide. Not every youngster with a mental illness, every kid with social trouble, every student with access to guns, nor every teenager exposed to violent media is a future school shooter. Thus, there has to be a combination of factors to prevail a teenager to shoot down his teachers and fellow classmates. Thus, one can say that it is like a big puzzle with lots of pieces to it.[39] Additionally, warning signs must be ignored by friends and family. Therefore, it is easy for the shooters to carry out their plans. However, one can only list the factors that may have led to the shootings. But yet, the final result is that no one can really say what prompts a teenager to perpetrate a mass murder at school. There is no register where one can check off warning signs indicating who is capable of committing a blood bath on a school-related stage.[40] In addition to this, many students also "remain well below radar range."[41] This means that many youngsters are able to hide their troubles and difficulties. And invisible warning signs cannot be detected by other people. Also, in advance, no one can expect a person to be aware of the reasons why a gunner perpetrates a carnage, when one does not even know in retrospect. Solely the shooters themselves might know what misdirected them. However, nobody can ask the perpetrators who committed suicide about their reasons. And the gunners who are still alive sometimes cannot name the factors that made them to the greatly feared teenagers that are known all over the world, because they hit the headlines with their deadly massacres.

---

[38] Cf. Appendix: Bowling For Columbine: Are we a nation of gun nuts or are we just nuts?
[39] Cf. Corliss, Richard. Bang, You're Dead (1999 Vol. 153 No. 17; pg. 50).
[40] Cf. FBI Academy. The School Shooter: A Threat Assessment Perspective (pg. 1).
[41] Cf. Newman, Katherine S. and Fox, Cybelle and Roth, Wendy (2002, pg. 110).

2.4 The Shooters

Often it was attempted to characterize shooters. Yet, a clear definition of a teenager who commits an attack on his or her own school does not exist.[42] However, one can to try validate the fact that there has to be a combination of factors for a student to commit carnage at an education place and, based on these results, one might be able to find main traits of gunners. In the following, this point is to be deduced on the basis of three samples. The first paradigm is Michael Carneal. When Michael was fourteen, he committed a school shooting

Michael Carneal[3]

in West Paducah, Kentucky. Armed with a .22-caliber Ruger pistol, which he had stolen from a neighbor, he entered the Heath High School on December 1, 1997. He killed a total of three students and wounded five.[43] Other than most troubled kids, Michael grew up with a stable family background. Yet, he always felt like he is not tantamount to his sister Kelly. He felt inferior since his sibling was well-liked and popular. Therefore, sibling tenseness arose. When Michael was circa seven years old, he decided to grow different.[44]

However, he never reached the same status as his sister.[45] Nevertheless, Michael's major problems were not family trouble, but social trouble at school. The teenager was bullied, teased and harassed at Heath High School. Aggravating the situation, he did not react against the assaults. In an inactive position he approved the behavior of his bullies. Also, he was incapable of talking to an adult about his predicament. Michael bottled up his anger and was only able to express his feelings in his writings.[46] Even the high school's headmaster "said [that] the boy's school essays and short stories revealed that he felt weak and picked on."[47] Even though, Michael was tormented, he was not a total outcast. Some fellow students viewed him as a friend counting him to "part of their inner circle."[48] Yet, Carneal tried to become friends with the wrinkly students. When the youngster tried to get involved in a Goth group, he became a difficult child himself. Michael started shoplifting and gave his yield to the group to increase his popularity. However, this did not work as well as he hoped it would.[49] Regardless of his misbehavior, Carneal never depicted the cliché-ridden embodiment of a troubled kid. With an intelligence quotient 120 he had a surpassing knowledgeability for his age. Yet, his grades were not good and, therefore, he had academic

[42] Cf. FBI Academy. The School Shooter: A Threat Assessment Perspective (pg. 1).
[43] Cf. Cloud, John. Just a Routine School Shooting (1999, Vol. 153 No. 21; pg. 34; pg. 36).
[44] Cf. Newman, Katherine S. and Fox, Cybelle and Roth, Wendy (2002, pg. 23 f.).
[45] Cf. Mendoza, Antonio (2002, pg. 77 f.).
[46] Cf. Newman, Katherine S. and Fox, Cybelle and Roth, Wendy (2002, pg. 26 f.).
[47] Cabell, Brian. Who is Michael Carneal? (18/01/2007).
[48] Newman, Katherine S. and Fox, Cybelle and Roth, Wendy (2002, pg. 25).
[49] Cf. Newman, Katherine S. and Fox, Cybelle and Roth, Wendy (2002, pg. 29).

trouble.[50] Also, he had a disciplinary record including downloading pornographic pictures from bodies of an Internet page. Still, Michael was not known as a troublemaker by the school's staff.[51] Notwithstanding, there were other apparent signs pointing at a school shooting besides bullying, sibling rivalry and straying from the right path. Michael was paranoid and had a persecution complex. He believed that demons haunted him and always felt spied on.[52] Also, in his pre-homicide days, he was diagnosed with depression.[53] Moreover, Michael was influenced by the media. He watched violent movies like 'Basketball Diaries' and played ego-shooter games like 'Doom'.[54] Comprising, one can say that Michael Carneal showed some main traits which can be interpreted as warning signs. He did not feel accepted in society, had a mental illness, was influenced by violent media and, despite his intelligence, he had some academic trouble. This paradigm also confirms the fact that there has to be a combination of factors and reasons to transform a student to a murderer. Another magnificent specimen is Andrew Golden. The child was aged eleven when he and his thirteen year old friend, Mitchell Johnson, committed their bloody deed. On March 24, 1998, the youngsters entered their

Andrew Golden[4]

school in Jonesboro, Arkansas, heavily armed. Their arsenal included three rifles and seven handguns which they had stolen from family members. The terrifying result of the shooting at Westside Middle School was the aggregate amount of ten wounded students, one dead teacher and four assassinated pupils.[55] Golden's case is an outlier. Firstly, he was really young when he committed his shooting and, furthermore, it is uncommon that teenage carnages are committed by more than one gunner.[56] Even though, this instance is a special case, the student shows some negative features of school shooters. For one thing, Andrew was a gun zealot and, even at his young age, an excellent marksman. Before he turned seven, he owned his own rifle and, since his family was just as gun fanatic as he was, he stole the firearms, which were used for the carnage, from his relatives.[57] Furthermore, the youngster was known to be evil. Neighbors and friends reported that Andrew did cruelty to animals and prided himself on slaying little creatures such as squirrels.[58] For these reasons, one can say that some conspicuous features of gunners in general are displayed by Andrew

[50] Cf. Newman, Katherine S. and Fox, Cybelle and Roth, Wendy (2002, pg. 24).
[51] Cf. Mendoza, Antonio (2002, pg. 75).
[52] Cf. Newman, Katherine S. and Fox, Cybelle and Roth, Wendy (2002, pg. 25).
[53] Cf. Mendoza, Antonio (2002, pg. 79).
[54] Cf. Cloud, John. Just a Routine School Shooting (1999, Vol. 153 No. 21; pg. 34; pg. 36).
[55] Cf. Cloud, John. Just a Routine School Shooting (1999, Vol. 153 No. 21; pg. 34; pg. 37).
[56] Cf. Lane, Brian and Gregg, Wilfred (2004, pg. 73).
[57] Cf. Newman, Katherine S. and Fox, Cybelle and Roth, Wendy (2002, pg. 39).
[58] Cf. Mendoza, Antonio (2002, pg. 102 f.).

Golden. He had a mean side which was evinced in aggressive and cruel behavior. Furthermore, he had a love for guns and access to the deadly weapons. Also, this particular case shows that a combination of factors is required for children to commit a schoolyard shooting. Moreover, this incident shows that even young kids are capable of doing terrible things. The third and final example is Jeff Weise. The sixteen-year old teenager committed the Red Lake shooting on March 21, 2005, in Northern Minnesota.[59] To get possession of some weapons, Weise killed his grandfather Daryl Lussier and Michelle Sigana, who was Lussier's girlfriend. After the murders he thieved a .40-caliber handgun and a 12-gauge shotgun. Heavily armed with the firearms he drove to his school to satisfy his desire to kill. Jeff slew seven fellow students and staff members of the Red Lake High School. All in all, he

Jeff Weise[5]

wounded many people and murdered nine humans before committing suicide.[60] The story hit the headlines. Not only because it was a school homicide, but because it all happened in an Indian reservation. The Red Lake High School is located in the "reservation of the proud Ojibawa Nation in Minnesota."[61] The reservation which is pinpointed in the northern part of the state is the asylum for one of the most beggarly folks of Minnesota, the Red Lake Chippewa Tribe. About 5000 people reside in the area. Among these are about one hundred Indians and three hundred pupils of the Red Lake High School.[62] Even though, Jeff Weise lived in the reservation, he was not a non-threatening child and,

therefore, shows some traits which could be typical for school shooters. Firstly, the teenager was mentally unstable and had an instable family background, too. The youngster's mother was in a motor accident in 1999. Subsequently, Jeff was sent to live with kinsmen since his mother sustained a fatal brain damage. Also, he was never really able to cope with his father's death who committed suicide in 1997. Thus, he did not talk about death to anyone in person, yet discussed the topic online. On a homepage he also talked about doing away with himself. However, he decided that it was not time to die yet and went on antidepressants. His labile situation was espoused by drinking vast quantities of alcohol and smoking marijuana.[63] For another thing, Weise sympathized with the National Socialist German Workers' Party. He

[59] Cf. Johnson, Jennifer Syltie. Troubled teen kills nine, and himself, at Red Lake (21/01/2007).
[60] Cf. Maag, Chris. The Devil in Red Lake (2005, Vol. 165 No. 14; pg. 35 ff.).
[61] Maag, Chris. The Devil in Red Lake (2005, Vol. 165 No. 14; pg. 36).
[62] Cf. Johnson, Jennifer Syltie. Troubled teen kills nine, and himself, at Red Lake (21/01/2007).
[63] Cf. Maag, Chris. The Devil in Red Lake (2005, Vol. 165 No. 14; pg. 36 f.).

published notes on a neo-nazi Web site, proclaiming his veneration for Adolf Hitler.[64] For the reasons which were mentioned, one can say that Jeff was negativly influenced by adverse media publications and had an instable frame of mind. The three examples indicate some features all shooters might have in common. Those attributes are influence by violent media, access to guns, being picked on and instable backgrounds. However, these indicators are not definite enough to draw up a characteristic of school shooters. Also, for different people, there have to be various reasons and factors. Withal, some teenagers are amenable to suggestions while others are not. In spite of that, the three paradigms exhibit that there is always more than one reason for a youngster to shoot at his fellow classmates and members of the school staff. Yet, it is hard to tell precisely when a teenager will snap and how fatal the combination of factors has to be. Also, the three samples show that different types of people are capable of committing school shootings.

3. Aftermaths of school rampages

3.1 How victims cope with the shootings

A school shooting always involves many victims. One can discern different types of affected people. The first group are the relatives and friends of the assassinated teachers and students. The course of reviving from the deprivation of a family member or a friend from slaying is tedious and difficult. Moreover, this process is hardly ever completely finished. The lives of the bereaved are changed forever, missing an important person in their existence. They have to live with grief and have to comprehend the Criminal Justice System which does not always bestow the justice the relatives and friends of the murdered demand. Also, the loss of a loved one because of murder is hard to accept since there is no rational reason for it.[65] Some parents tried to deal with their pain by writing books. The most famous of those books is "Rachel's Tears: The Spiritual Journey of Columbine Martyr Rachel Scott" which was published on behalf of Rachel Scott's parents just shortly after she was killed.[66] Rachel was a Columbine victim. The well-liked girl was assassinated by Dylan Klebold and Eric Harris when she was only aged seventeen.[67] The book is a story about the life, death and faith of the Columbine victim narrated by her folks and portrayed in her own words by

---

[64] Cf. Johnson, Jennifer Syltie. Troubled teen kills nine, and himself, at Red Lake (21/01/2007).
[65] Cf. O'Hara, Jean. Coping with the violent death of a loved one (19/01/2007).
[66] Cf. Keating, Mary Ellen. Rachel's Tears: The Spiritual Journey of Columbine Martyr Rachel Scott (20/01/2007).
[67] Cf. Gibbs, Nancy. ...In Sorrow and Disbelief (1999, Vol. 153 No. 17; pg. 31).

drawings from Rachel's own diaries. The Columbine shooters aimed at killing the young girl. This became obvious since the shooters made fun of her Christian faith on a few self-made video recordings before. Henceforth, everyone can read the explanation of her mother and her father how they were able to accept their daughter's death after understanding the denotation in Rachel's martyrdom. The Scotts try to manage their own pain and grief. However, they also attempt to give hope to others who suffered from school violence.[68] Another group involved in the shootings are the attesters who witnessed the bloody deeds. Beyond the pain of losing fellow classmates and colleagues, they have to deal with what they have experienced. Many eyewitnesses are traumatized after they suffered during the shootings. After a shocker like a school carnage the same film gets replayed over and over again in the mind of a victim. That is what doctors call a trauma. No one, who is concerned, is able to get rid of the terrible memories.[69] This happens since the human brain does not know how to process all the brutal impressions. However, this would be necessary to handle a trauma. If the trauma-causing experience remains untreated, even little attractions can cause the body to shift into an anxiety state. Such a behavior can derogate a victim's life. Therefore, it is recommended to consult a doctor. It is the task of therapists to support people to put the shocking memories behind themselves.[70] Since traumatized people tend to avoid similar situations, it is very important to help the affected students and teachers. Otherwise they would not be able to go back to school.[71] After the school homicide in Germany, different measures were taken to help the pupils to cope with their experiences. It is said that all the children were afraid of the school building and were disconcerted about their own future. The most important sanction in this stage was not to treat individuals, but to support the group since solidarity strengthened everyone. Also, it was important that the auxiliaries were the towers of strength for the victims. The helpers had to prompt the affected students and teachers to talk about the experienced situations. It was also vital that the aids explained to the victims that crying and sitting listlessly is alright.[72] Overall, everything pointed at two main necessities. The parties involved needed someone to listen and require social cohesion and strong company. Those things do not make the happenings undone, yet it makes the situation more bearable. In addition, there are people that do not only suffer mentally from the shootings but also physically. On top of losing friends or colleagues and witnessing the entire shooting, the wounded are injured. Examples of such an aggrieved party are the

---

[68] Cf. Keating, Mary Ellen. Rachel's Tears: The Spiritual Journey of Columbine Martyr Rachel Scott (20/01/2007).
[69] Cf. Schächter, Markus. Traumata: nach dem Schock ist das Gehirn hilflos: Die Betroffenen haben das Bild des schrecklichen Erlebnisses vor Augen (20/01/2007).
[70] Cf. Schächter, Markus. Wie ein Horrorfilm, der wieder und wieder abläuft: Taumata entstehen, weil das Gehirn die Erinnerungen nicht zusammenfügen kann (20/01/2007).
[71] Cf. Schächter, Markus. Traumata: nach dem Schock ist das Gehirn hilflos: Die Betroffenen haben das Bild des schrecklichen Erlebnisses vor Augen (20/01/2007).
[72] Sadigh, Parvin. Verletzte Seelen (20/01/2007).

victims Richard Castaldo and Mark Taylor. Both of the former Columbine students appeared in the movie "Bowling for Columbine: Are we a nation of gun nuts or are we just nuts". Richard was shot several times with a TEC 9mm semi-automatic pistol and is now paraplegic and wheelchair-bound. Mark needed several operations till he was able to walk again. He was shot repeatedly, too. He still has a bullet between his main artery and his spinal column and another slug just an inch away from his aorta. The Columbine shooting left the two former students as cripples and lined through their injuries.[73] Taylor was incredibly lucky to survive, because the

Richard Castaldo[6]

bullets had penetrated his entire body. The teenager tried to cope with his hard fate with his believe in God.[74] Richard Castaldo talked about his situation five years after the massacre in an interview with the television station MTV. He is living a normal life studying business and residing on his own. However, he still has to live with the consequences of the bloody Columbine massacre. Other than being lamed, he has trouble with his hand. He was going to a hand therapist for some time. During the shooting, some nerves in his left arm were damaged. Even though his hand is almost back to normal, one of his fingers is still aggrieved. Anyhow, Richard is still hopeful that some physician will find a therapy or a cure for his medulla damage. In spite of that, he hates the fact that some things take him way longer than they used to before he was paralyzed. He thinks that he will never get totally used to it, because it annoys him every once in a while.[75] All in all, the victims all have to suffer from the shootings for the rest of their lives. For one thing, the bereaved might need years to get over the death of their relatives, friends or colleagues. Also, eyewitnesses always have to spend a long time on surmounting the difficulties they have after they experienced something as cold-blooded as a school shooting. Moreover, the injured might be aggrieved to the end of their lives. For all who are personally affected the teenage rampage is more than a story that hit the headlines. For them it is the day that changed everything. It is a memory the victims cannot forget about. However, everyone of them has to find a way to cope with the occurred.

---

[73] Cf. Moore, Michael. Bowling For Columbine: Are we a nation of gun nuts or are we just nuts? (Scene 18).
[74] Cf. Ensslin, John C. Columbine victim: Faith saved my life (20/01/2007).
[75] Fraenkel, Jim and Scorca, Shari. Columbine High, Five Years Later (20/01/2007).

3.2 What became of the shooters

Barry Loukaitis[7]

For the shooters the day of their rampage is the date that changed everything, as well. Many shooters either committed suicide or got shot committing so-called suicide by cops. The most famous examples are Eric Harris and Dylan Klebold, the two Columbine shooters.[76] Also, the German student Robert Steinhäuser killed himself with a self-inflicted gunshot after killing thirteen teachers and a policeman at his grammar school in Erfurt.[77] However, other gunners have been arrested. Amongst them is Barry Loukaitis, who killed one teacher and two students and wounded another fellow classmate on Feb 2, 1996, at Frontier Junior High in Moses Lake, Washington. The teenager, who was fourteen at that time, is now serving two life sentences at the Clallam Bay Correction Center.[78] Also, Loukaitis has no option of parole.[79] Similarly, Michael Carneal, who committed the shooting in West Paducah, Kentucky, is now severing a life sentence.[80] The teenager has no chance of parole for twenty-five years since he was plead 'guilty but mentally ill' and is now treated for his insanity at a mental establishment.[81] A Time Magazine article reveals that he hardly has any visitors and, therefore is lonely.[82] Yet, other children who assassinated their teachers and classmates were not sentenced to life. Andrew Golden and Mitchell Johnson, the two Westside shooters, can be adduce as an instance. Since the two killers were younger than fourteen they could not be sentenced to more than confinement until age twenty-one. Both teenagers received the maximum punishment and were compelled to live in a state youth facility. However, this implied that Johnson was freed on August 11, 2005, and Golden will be released on his twenty-first birthday on May 25, 2007.[83] American society was shocked by the release of the school shooter since Mitchell does not even have a criminal record now. "He could even legally, if he chose to, buy a gun."[84] If justice is served with any of these sentences is questionable since there can never be an ample justice for a dead child, friend or sibling.

---

[76] Cf. Ferro, Jeffery (2001, pg. 98).
[77] Cf. Lane, Brian and Gregg, Wilfred (2004, pg. 317).
[78] Cf. Cloud, John. Just a Routine School Shooting (1999, Vol. 153 No. 21; pg. 34; pg. 36).
[79] Cf. Mendoza, Antonio (2002, pg. 41).
[80] Cf. Cloud, John. Just a Routine School Shooting (1999, Vol. 153 No. 21; pg. 34; pg. 36).
[81] Cf. Mendoza, Antonio (2002, pg. 82 f.).
[82] Cf. Roche, Timothy and Bower, Amanda. Young voices from cell pg. 2 (08/08/2006).
[83] Cf. Mendoza, Antonio (2002, pg. 105 f.).
[84] Williams, Pete. Jonesboro school shooter free after seven years (19/01/2007).

3.3 The copycat effect

School shootings have a threatening effect on society, because they offer a new problem. Big headlines inspire other teenagers to copy the homicides. In particular, youngsters with trouble are attracted by such a load of attention. Especially after the Columbine shootings the number of threats and attacks on school-related stages rose. There are two different reasons for copycats to imitate a crime. For one thing, they have thought about violent acts before and were beating about for a hint on how to commit a malefaction efficiently. This is the so-called mode copying. In the second place, most copycats are decoyed by the pure agitation of making catch lines. Imitators think that committing a notorious crime is a good and fast way to acquire importance.[85] Roger Ebert once explained his point of view very apposite in a news show. He stated that if school shootings are influenced by anything, they "are influenced by news programs [..]. Cable news drops ordinary programming and goes around the clock with [the news about the shooting]. The message is clear to other disturbed kids around the country: If I shoot up my school, I can be famous."[86] Other youngsters, who do not have anything to lose, view a schoolyard shooting as their last resort. Unfortunately, it is questionable if the copycat effect can be stopped. It is unconvertible to keep deadly shootings out of the news programs. Also, the main problem is not the news coverage. The central problem is that emulators do not realize that they are responsible for any consequences following the shooting. The perpetrators ruin their future lives.[87] "That's the part of the story few copycats have in mind while daydreaming of their moment in the spotlight."[88]

4. Prevention methods

4.1 Gun Control

School massacres always raise the topic of gun control closely linked to the "American gun culture."[89] Many people believe that reducing the access to weapons would stop shooters from committing schoolyard homicides. They presume that diminishing the gun availability is going to lower the causes of gun violence among teenagers at school.[90] There are different

---

[85] Cf. Cohen, Adam. Criminals as Copycats (1999 Vol. 153 No. 21; pg. 38).
[86] Borenstein, David. Quoteland...All the right words (24/01/2007).
[87] Cf. Cohen, Adam. Criminals as Copycats (1999 Vol. 153 No. 21; pg. 38).
[88] Cohen, Adam. Criminals as Copycats (1999 Vol. 153 No. 21; pg. 38).
[89] Morrow, Lance. Coming to Clarity About Guns (1999 Vol. 153 No. 17; pg. 46).
[90] Cf. "The School Shootings: Are Guns to Blame?." Issues & Controversies On File 29 May 1998.

standpoints approaching this subject. Firstly, some gun activists believe that things concerning gun safety have to alter. Firearms are often "carelessly stored in the parental home or home of a friend or relative"[91] and supply the shooters with weaponries. Some states in America adopted the 'Child Access Prevention' law. Florida was the first state to introduce this act in 1989. One commits an offence when repositing or leaving a charged up gun in the scope of a minor. Therefore, gun owners are forced to cordon off their weapons. Tragic stories coming forth from the careless custody of guns have gone back ever since the 'Child Access Prevention' law was passed. However, so far only nineteen states put the bill through.[92] But for all that, it is still questionable if this statute keeps a teenager from gaining access to a gun by breaking a lock. The second attitude toward gun control is that schools should control students and search them for weapons. Gun activists believe that controllers should be introduced at schools with the function of a daily inspection of pupils.[93] However, this measure is just not practical. And besides, other people take the view that guns are not the reason for school shootings. The biggest group which presses this point is the National Rifle Association. The union relies on the fact that in austerely controlled countries such as Germany, the rate of gun-related malefactions is a far bit higher than in nations with looser regulations.[94] Defiant of the National Rifle Association's dedication for more liberty concerning gun control, policymakers made some changes which restrict the freedom of weapon owners. One month after the Columbine massacre, the Senate passed one of the most fundamental proposals concerning gun-control. This registration included a background checkup for weapon purchasers at gun shows.[95] Yet, agreements like this one are always hard to find. In the first ballot "when the votes were counted, the 100 Senators had split evenly."[96] Generally, one can say that gun laws in the United States are hard to change since the Second Amendment of the Bill of Rights amounts: "A well regulated militia, being necessary to the security of a free state, the right of the people to keep and bear arms, shall not be infringed."[97] Based on this amendment many Americans substantiate their right to own guns and carry firearms. And it is a fact that the majority of the politicians hardly ever support basic changes which could disaffect their voters.

---

[91] Carter, Green Lee (2002, pg. 521).
[92] Cf. Hamm, Peter and Ragbourn, Zach. Child Access Prevention (CAP) Laws and Gun Owned Responsibility – Frequently Asked Questions (06/01/2007).
[93] Cf. Williams, Frank P. and McShane, Marilyn D. (2003, pg. 335).
[94] Cf. National Rifle Association of America, Institute For Legislative Action. Gun Laws, Culture, Justice and Crime in Foreign Countries (10/01/2007).
[95] Cf. Novak, Viveca. Picking a Fight with the N.R.A. (1999 Vol. 153 No. 21; pg. 54).
[96] Carney, James and Dickerson, John F. Political Gunplay (1999, Vol. 153 No. 21; pg. 53).
[97] Cornell University Law School. United States Constitution: Bill of Rights (23/01/2007).

4.2 Restrictions of violent media

There have been heated controversies about the restriction of violent media after schoolyard schootings. Yet, only a few changes have been made over the last years. Those modifications are mainly regulations which are in force only in single states. As such an example the requirement for merchants to display a notification of a rating system, which was put into effect in Michigan, Georgia, Washington and California over the past few years, can be listed.[98] However, there have been considerably more legislative proposals concerning violent media than laws were passed. Most filed application only came up for hearings but the discussions never came to a conclusion. Opposers of registration laws for violence in media lean onto the following facts. Firstly, it is a written down law that the parents are expected to supervise the actions of their offspring. They are supposed to occupy their kids with good activities and keep them away from violence. Furthermore, laws terminating a youngster's approachability to tobacco, guns, alcohol, gambling, and pornography were introduced because it is proved that those doings risk minor teenagers. Yet, there has been no scientific evidence that violence in television, videos, games and internet pages are harming children, it is only said that those things might be damnifying.[99] All the same, it is questionable if it is enough to have children only supervised by their parents. They can not observe their children twenty-four hours a day. Therefore, it is comprehensible that many people demand stricter laws regulating the retail and the dispersiveness of violent media.

4.3 What schools can do

Since schools were blamed to be too large and, ipso facto, too impersonal there must be things they can change for the better. For one thing, lowering the schools' sizes is suggested. If a school is smaller, it grants teachers and students the opportunity to know each other better. Also, in a diminutive school there is less competition. It is easier to join bands, sport teams and other extracurricular activities. Therefore, there are fewer outsiders since it is easier for kids to fit in. Also, the fact that there are fewer students per teacher makes it easier to spot warning signs. Even former Vice President, Al Gore, stated that it is impossible to detect early signs of violence among teenagers, depression and scholastic miscarriage in a stodged school. In addition, research exhibits that students of smaller schools receive better grades. Moreover, they are less likely to be embrangled in brawls and

---

[98] Cf. Child-Responsible Media Campaign. A Summary of Violent Media Legislation in the United States (22/01/2007).
[99] Cf. Walsh, David. Video Game Violence and Public Policy (22/01/2007).

caboodles because they know that someone is always monitoring them. Also, students from small schools are more willing to discuss their problems with teachers and administrators. Additionally, they attend class more regularly, are less likely to drop out and tend to participate more often in school activities. Even though, the cost per student at small schools might be higher than at bigger schools, it is an investment which is worth the expense. There is a human gain that one can not balance out with money.[100] Furthermore, the lack of administration was criticized on schools.[101] To solve these problems, more teachers and administrators could be hired. In 1999, a mean school district did not have enough psychologists for all the demanding students.[102] Yet, this costs a lot of money and it is questionable if this is a measure which can be implemented. Besides, there are different actions which an advisory board named "Fight Crime" has developed. The plan suggests four points to prevent school violence. One of those points approaches education places in particular. It is recommended to "help schools to identify troubled kids early and provide counseling for them."[103] Some school already responded to the school shootings and introduced some steps to detect difficult children sooner. The first step school officials have to take is to examine the commonness of threats, violent acts and other crimes on a schoolyard. Since police reports only cover the incidents which are advised to the police, they are not detailed enough to behold the dimension of school felonies. The same problem can be seen when studying official reports. They only cover the occurrences which were reported to the school administration. Therefore, surveys must also help officials to evaluate the situation. A survey conducted by the school board, questioning teachers and students, can support the validation for the climate within the school. Yet, just like with other questionnaires one has to be careful when analyzing the results. They depend on the number of the sample and substance of the replies. An in depth study of the surveys, official and police reports can offer an accurate view on how precarious the situation of a school is. Thus, expose how well school crime prevention methods and strategies work. Also, a physical appraisal should be carried out at every school.[104] This "physical security assessment should include the number and location of entrances and exits, lighting around the buildings and parking lots, and inventory control."[105] After this examination, school officials have to decide whether a security staff has to be introduced or not.[106] Also, some education places experiment with different safety precautions which were developed in prisons for juvenile delinquent. Those cautionary measures include metal detectors and

---

[100] Cf. Christian, Nichole. Is Smaller Perhaps Better? (1999 Vol. 153 No. 21; pg. 43).
[101] Cf. Carter, Green Lee (2002, pg. 522).
[102] Cf. Cloud, John. What Can the Schools Do? (1999 Vol. 153 No. 17; pg. 40).
[103] Cloud, John. What Can the Schools Do? (1999 Vol. 153 No. 17; pg. 39 f.).
[104] Cf. Williams, Frank P. and McShane, Marilyn D. (2003, pg. 336).
[105] Williams, Frank P. and McShane, Marilyn D. (2003, pg. 336).
[106] Cf. Williams, Frank P. and McShane, Marilyn D. (2003, pg. 336).

observation cameras.[107] Yet, schools have to give a wide berth to jail-like ambiences. Educational establishments should not turn into borstals but should be pleasant everyday peripheries for young people to attain knowledge.[108] Therefore, a balance between strict control and blatant ignorance has to be struck. Another advocated measure is the indoctrination of the school staffs. They should better their expertise in the departments concerning "discipline, classroom management, and conflict mediation."[109] Precise precepts for malfunction will contribute to upgrade the school climate.[110] It will never be possible to foreclose every sign of violence, bullying and assault at schools, yet it is worth while trying to improve the climate at the education places of pupils.

5. Conclusion

Concluding, one can ascertain the following things. Firstly, there have been many fatal and shocking school shootings in the past. Most of those carnages took place in the United States, yet teenage homicides occur in other countries, too. The fact, that there is no certainty that school shootings are going to vanish into thin air in the foreseeable future, is horrifying. Also, it is worrying that there is no list where one can check off warning signs which indicate who is capable of committing a blood bath on a school-related stage. Therefore, one cannot pick out potential school shooters. Yet, everyone is capable of making schools safer. When being attentive, one can detect warning signs and, thus, gunners could be stop before they put their deadly plans into action. Besides, some measures were taken to contain the access to guns and lower the influence of violent media on teenagers. However, no one knows if this is going to be enough to prohibit school massacres in the future. It is to be hoped that not too many teenagers stray from the right path and perpetrate school shootings. For an onlooker it is difficult to understand the enormity of a school shooting. However, for the affected people a school homicide is more than a news story. Also, for them the events do not end when the news coverage stops. They have to live their lives with the consequences and horrible memories of the carnages. Yet, there is one thing everyone can do. To express it in Brooks Browns words, people have to "learn from the injustice of Columbine. Look for where parallels are happening elsewhere. [...] Then fight to change it. Don't wait for everyone else. Don't let the world happen around you. Don't stay powerless. Don't give up."[111]

---

[107] Cf. Cloud, John. What Can the Schools Do? (1999 Vol. 153 No. 17; pg. 39).
[108] Cf. Carter, Green Lee (2002, pg. 522).
[109] Williams, Frank P. and McShane, Marilyn D. (2003, pg. 336).
[110] Cf. Williams, Frank P. and McShane, Marilyn D. (2003, pg. 336).
[111] Brooks, Brown and Merritt, Rob (2002, pg. 270).

6. Appendix

"Rampage: The Social Roots of School Shootings" pg. 51

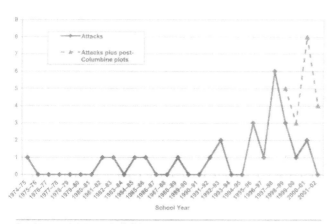

Figure 3.1   Number of School Shootings by School Year

Moore, Michael, <u>Bowling for Columbine: Are we a nation of gun nuts or are we just nuts?</u> (Chapter 7)
→ Interview with Marilyn Manson about the assumptions that he was responsible for the Columbine shootings

[...]

Marilyn Manson: I definitely can see why they would pick me. Because I think it's easy to throw my face on a TV, because in the end, I'm a poster boy for fear. Because I represent what everyone is afraid of, because I do and say whatever I want.

The two by-products, of that whole tragedy, were violence in entertainment and gun control. And how perfect that that was the two things that we were going to talk about with the upcoming election. And also, then we forgot about Monica Lewinsky and we forgot about, the President was shooting bombs overseas, yet I'm a bad guy because I sing some rock-and-roll songs, and who's a bigger influence, the President or Marilyn Manson? I'd like to think me, but I'm going to go with the President.

Michael Moore: Do you know that on the day of the Columbine happened, the US dropped more bombs on Kosovo than any other day?

Marilyn Manson: I do know that, and I think that's really ironic, that nobody said 'well maybe the President had an influence on this violent behavior' Because that's not the way the media wants to take it and spin it, and turn it into fear, because then you're watching television, you're watching the news, you're being pumped full of fear, there's floods, there's AIDS, there's murder, cut to commercial, buy the Acura, buy the Colgate, if you have bad breath they're not going to talk to you, if you have pimples, the girl's not going to fuck you, and it's just this campaign of fear, and consumption, and that's what I think it's all based on, the whole idea of 'keep everyone afraid, and they'll consume.' [...]

Michael Moore: If you were to talk directly to the kids at Columbine or the people in that community, what would you say to them if they were here right now?

Marilyn Manson: I wouldn't say a single word to them, I would listen to what they have to say and that's what no one did.

7. Bibliography

7.1 Books

Brooks, Brown and Merritt, Rob. No Easy Answers: The Truth Behind Death at Columbine. New York: Lantern Books, 2002.

Carter, Green Lee. Guns in American Society: An Encyclopedia of History, Politics, Culture, and the Law. Volume II: M-Z. Santa Barbara: ABC Clio, 2002.

Ferro, Jeffery. Gun Control: Restricting Rights or Protecting people? Farmington: Gale Group, 2001.

Lane, Brian and Gregg, Wilfred. The Encyclopedia of Mass Murder: A Chilling Record of the World's Worst Cases. London: Constable & Robinson, 2004.

Mendoza, Antonio. Teenage Rampage: The Worldwide Youth Crime Explosion. London: Virgin Books, 2002.

Newman, Katherine S. and Fox, Cybelle and Roth, Wendy. Rampage: The Social Roots of School Shootings. New York: Basic Books, 2005.

Williams, Frank P. and McShane, Marilyn D.. Encyclopedia of Juvenile Justice. Thousand Oaks; Sage Publication, 2003.

7.2 Articles

"The School Shootings: Are Guns to Blame?" Issues & Controversies On File May 29, 1998. Issues & Controversies @ FACTS.com. Facts on File News Services. 18. Apr. 2006 <http://2facts.com>.

7.3 Time Magazine Articles

Carney, James and Dickerson, John F. Political Gunplay. May 31, 1999 Vol. 153 No. 21; pg. 53, 2 pgs.

Christian, Nichole. Is Smaller Perhaps Better?. May 31, 1999 Vol. 153 No. 21; pg. 43.

Cohen, Adam. A Curse of Cliques. May 3, 1999 Vol. 153 No. 17; pg. 44; 2 pgs.

Cohen, Adam. Criminals as Copycats. May 31, 1999 Vol. 153 No. 21; pg. 38.

Cloud, John. Just a Routine School Shooting. May 31, 1999 Vol. 153 No. 21; pg. 34; 10 pgs.

Cloud, John. What Can the Schools Do?. May 3, 1999 Vol. 153 No. 17; pg. 38; 3 pgs.

Corliss, Richard. Bang, You're Dead. May 3, 1999 Vol. 153 No. 17; pg. 49; 2 pgs.

Dickinson, Amy. Where Were the Parents?. May 3, 1999 Vol. 153 No. 17; pg. 40.

Ferguson, Andrew. What Politicians Can't Do. May 3, 1999 Vol. 153 No. 17; pg. 52.

Gibbs, Nancy. ...In Sorrow and Disbelief. May 3, 1999 Vol. 153 No. 17; pg. 24; 13 pgs.

Gibbs, Nancy. TIME Special Report. May 31, 1999 Vol. 153 No. 21; pg. 33.

Maag, Chris. The Devil in Red Lake. April 4, 2005 Vol. 165 No. 14; pg. 35, 3 pgs.

Morrow, Lance. Coming to Clarity About Guns. May 3, 1999 Vol. 153 No. 17; pg. 46.

Novak, Viveca. Picking a Fight with the N.R.A. May 31, 1999 Vol. 153 No. 21; pg. 54.

Taylor, Chris. Digital Dungeons. May 3, 1999 Vol. 153 No. 17; pg. 50.

7.4 Videos

Moore, Michael. <u>Bowling for Columbine: Are we a nation of gun nuts or are we just nuts?</u>
2002.

7.5 Homepages

Borenstein, David
http://quoteland.com/author.asp?AUTHOR_ID=1553. Quoteland...All the right words;
(24/01/2007)

Cabell, Brian
http://www.cnn.com/US/9712/03/school.shooting.pm/. Who is Michael Carneal?: Sheriff says
school shooter may not have acted alone; (18/01/2007)

Child-Responsible Media Campaign
http://www.medialegislation.org/A%20Summary%20of%20Violent%20Media%20Legislation
%20in%20the%20United%20States.htm. A Summary of Violent Media Legislation in the
United States; (22/01/2007)

Cornell University Law School
http://www.law.cornell.edu/constitution/constitution.billofrights.html#amendmentii. United
States Constitution: Bill of Rights; (23/01/2007)

Embar, Wanda
http://veganpeace.com/gun_control/GunAvailability.htm. Gun availability; 10/01/2007.

Ensslin, John C.
http://www.denver-rmn.com/shooting/0127tayl4.shtml. Columbine victim: Faith saved my life;
(20/01/2007)

Fraenkel, Jim and Scorca, Shari
http://www.mtv.com/bands/c/columbine_anniversary/news_feature_042004/. Columbine
High, Five Years Later; (20/01/2007)

Hamm, Peter (Communications Director) and Ragbourn, Zach (Assistant Director) http://www.bradycampaign.org/facts/faqs/?page=cap. Child Access Prevention (CAP) Laws and Gun Owned Responsibility: Frequently Asked Questions; 06/01/2007.

Johnson, Jennifer Syltie (Vice President) http://news.minnesota.publicradio.org/features/2005/03/21_gundersond_redlakeshooting/. Troubled teen kills nine, and himself, at Red Lake; (21/01/2007)

Keating, Mary Ellen (Senior Vice President of Barnes and Nobles) http://search.barnesandnoble.com/booksearch/isbnInquiry.asp?z=y&EAN=9780785268482&i tm=1. Rachel's Tears: The Spiritual Journey of Columbine Martyr Rachel Scott; (20/01/2007)

National Rifle Association of America, Institute For Legislative Action http://www.nraila.org/Issues/FactSheets/Read.aspx?ID=78. Gun Laws, Culture, Justice and Crime in Foreign Countries; 10/01/2007.

O'Hara, Jean http://www.survivorsofmurdervictims.com/page779.html. Coping with the violent death of a loved one; (19/01/2007)

Pleitgen, Fritz http://www.wdr.de/themen/panorama/21/schule_emsdetten/index.jhtml. Emsdetten: Amoklauf war lange geplant; 06/01/2007.

Polizei Minden-Lübbecke http://www.paderzeitung.de/index.php?option=com_content&task=view&id=5236&Itemid=20 2. Trittbrettfahrer nach Amoklauf von Emsdetten beschäftigten auch die Polizei in Minden; 06/01/2007.

Roche, Timothy and Bower, Amanda http://www.time.com/time/nation/article/0,8599,127231,00.html. Young Voices from the Cell; 08/08/2006.

Sadigh, Parvin http://nurtext.zeit.de/online/2006/47/Emsdetten-Betreuung. Verletzte Seelen; (20/01/2007)

28

Schächter, Markus (Intendant)
http://www.3sat.de/3sat.php?http://www.3sat.de/nano/astuecke/65308/index.html. Wie ein
Horrorfilm, der wieder und wieder abläuft: Taumata entstehen, weil das Gehirn die
Erinnerungen nicht zusammenfügen kann; (20/01/2007)

Schächter, Markus (Intendant)
http://www.3sat.de/3sat.php?http://www.3sat.de/nano/astuecke/65308/index.html. Traumata:
nach dem Schock ist das Gehirn hilflos: Die Betroffenen haben das Bild des schrecklichen
Erlebnisses vor Augen; (20/01/2007)

Tompkins, Aimee
http://allpsych.com/journal/violentmedia.html. The Psychological Effects of Violent Media on
Children; 07/01/2007.

Walsh, David
http://culturalpolicy.uchicago.edu/conf2001/papers/walsh.html. Video Game Violence and
Public Policy; (22/01/2007)

Williams, Pete
http://www.msnbc.msn.com/id/8917466/. Jonesboro school shooter free after seven years:
Johnson, who just turned 21 years old, walks out with no criminal record; 19/01/2007.

7.6 PDF Data

FBI Academy. The School Shooter: A Threat Assessment Perspective. Editor: Isaacs,
Arnold.

7.7 Pictures

Picture 1 – Eric Harris and Dylan Klebold
http://images.usatoday.com/news/_photos/2006/07/06/journal2.jpg.

Picture 2 – Robert Steinhäuser
http://news.bbc.co.uk/olmedia/1950000/images/_1954668_killer150.jpg.

Picture 3 – Michael Carneal

http://www.crimelibrary.com/graphics/photos/serial_killers/history/pomeroy/1b.jpg.

Picture 4 – Andrew Golden

http://www.animalpeoplenews.org/gifs/andrew_golden.jpg.

Picture 5 – Jeff Weise

http://msnbcmedia.msn.com/j/msnbc/Components/Photos/050323/050323_jeff_weise_vmed 12p.h2.jpg.

Picture 6 – Richard Castaldo

http://www.imdb.com/gallery/ss/0310793/Ss/0310793/bowling_for_columbine_6.jpg.html?pat h=gallery&path_key=0310793.

Picture 7 – Barry Loukaitis

http://www.wackymurder.com/loukaitis.htm.

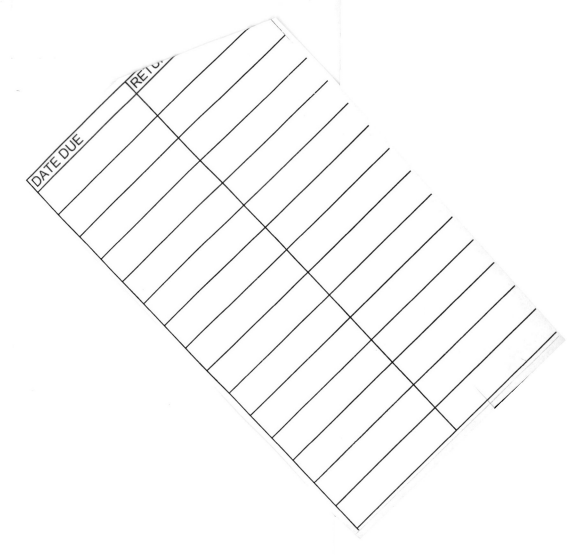

DATE DUE | RET...

CPSIA information can be obtained at www.ICGtesting.com
Printed in the USA
LVOW08s0902181114

414216LV00006B/353/P